Influence
the
energy.
You are
a whole
vibe sis.

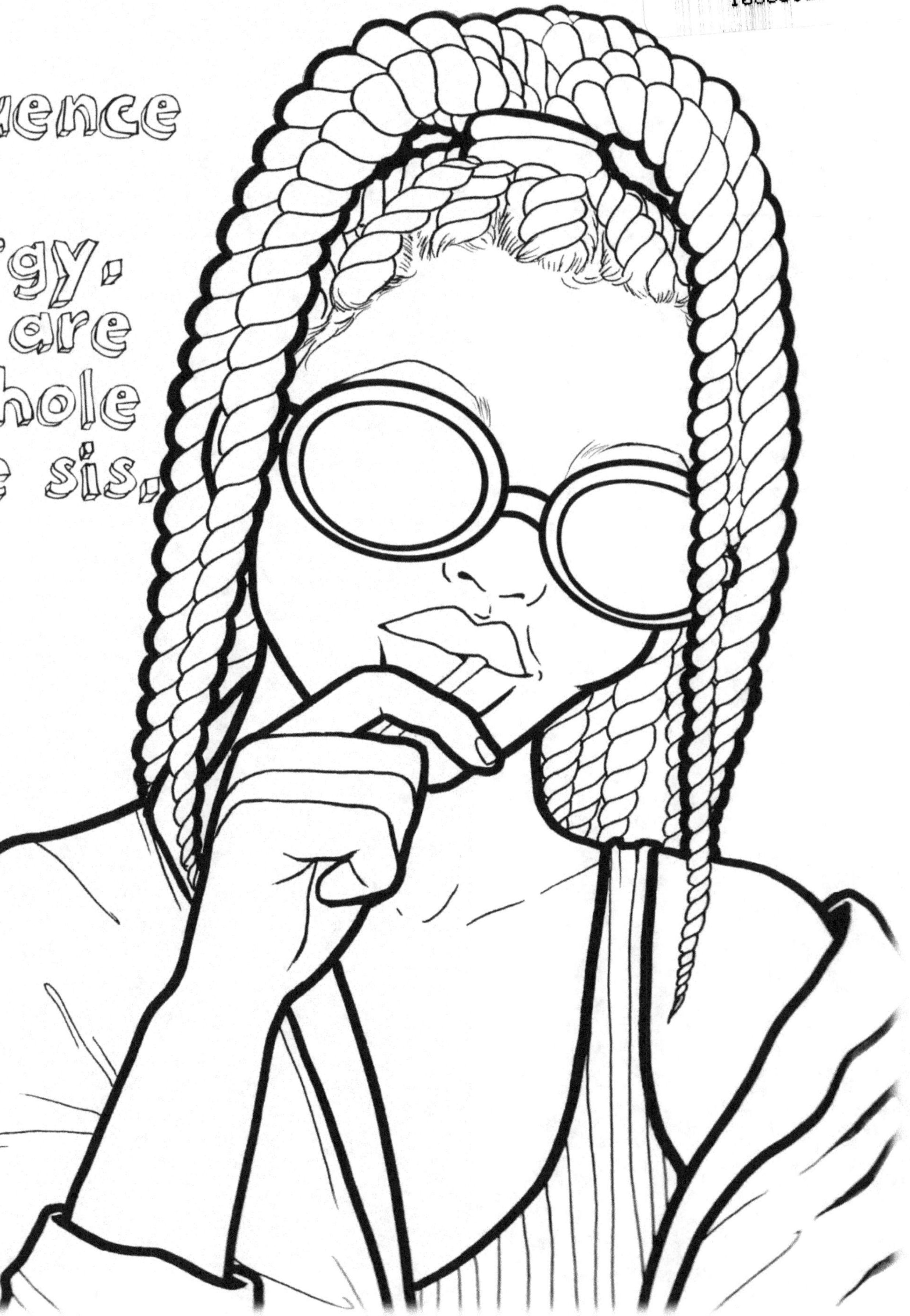

Fall in love with yourself

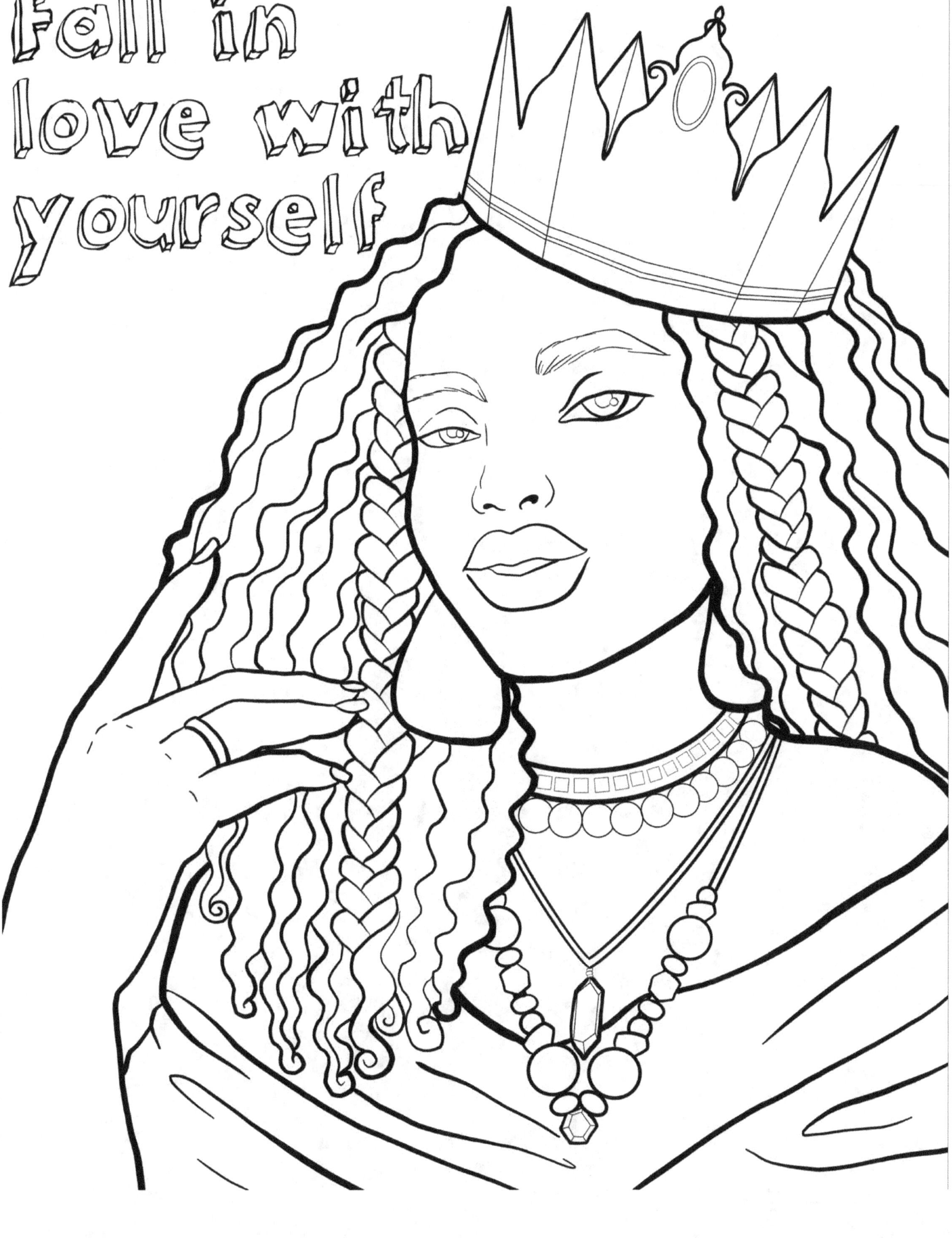

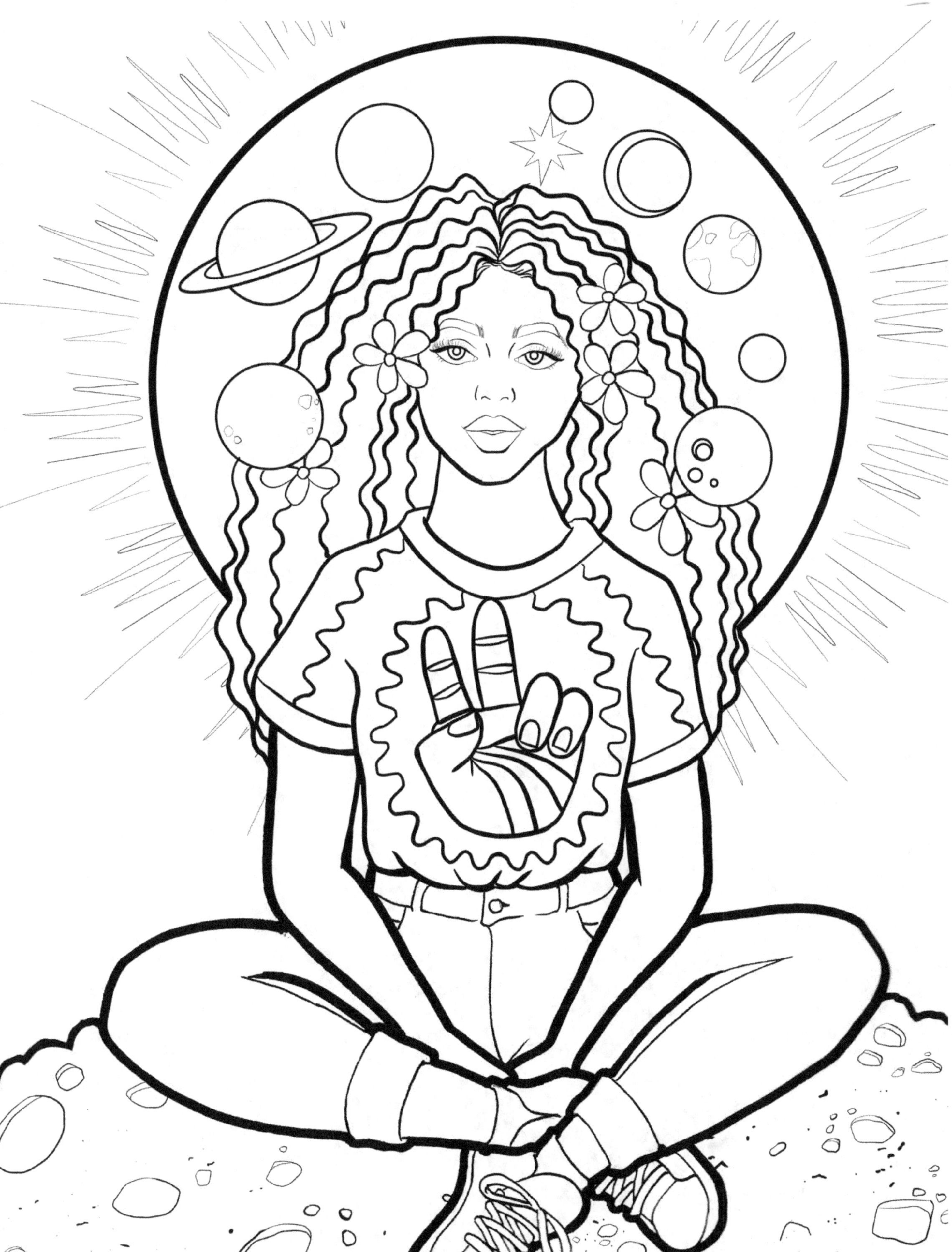

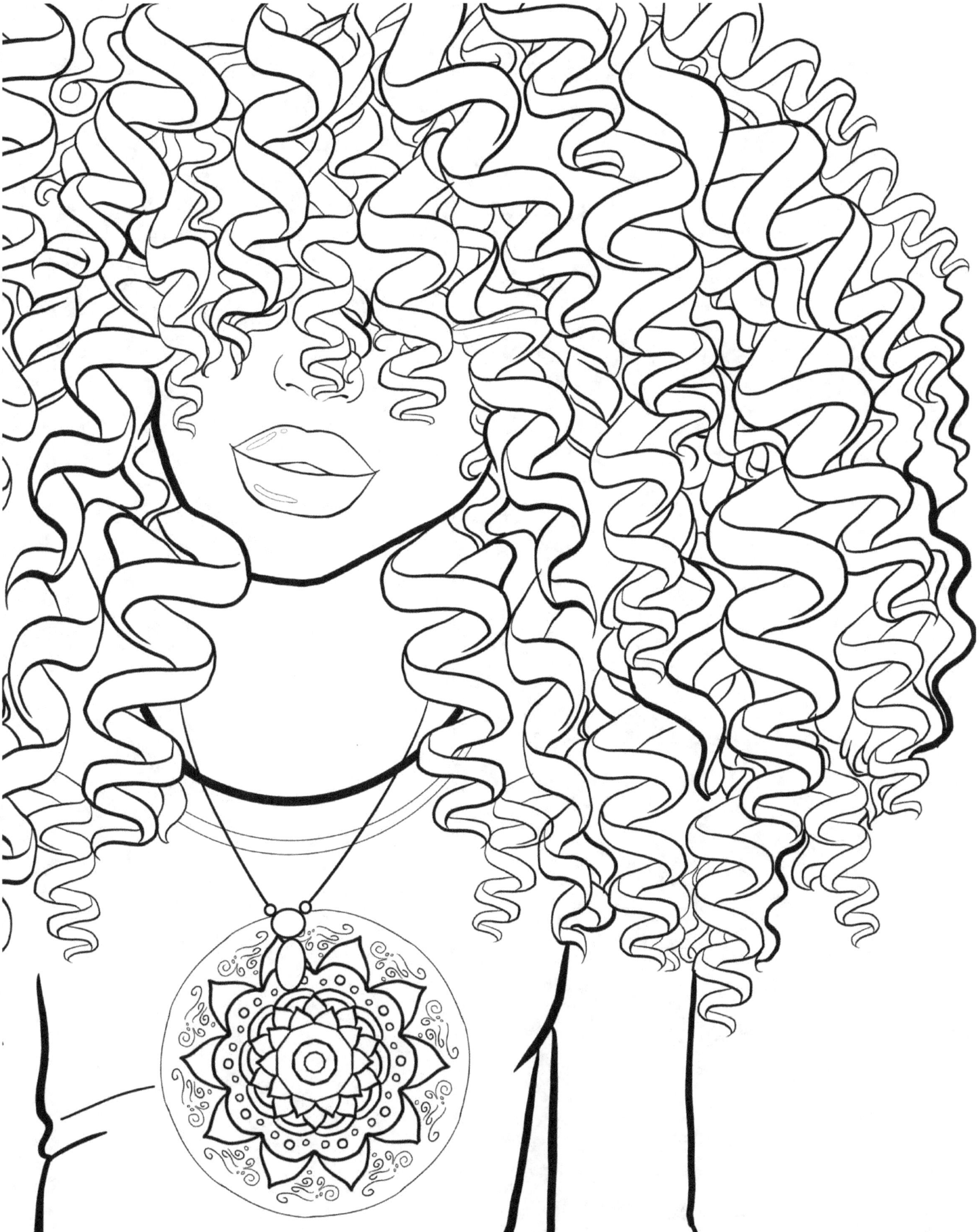

Shine
Bright
Queen

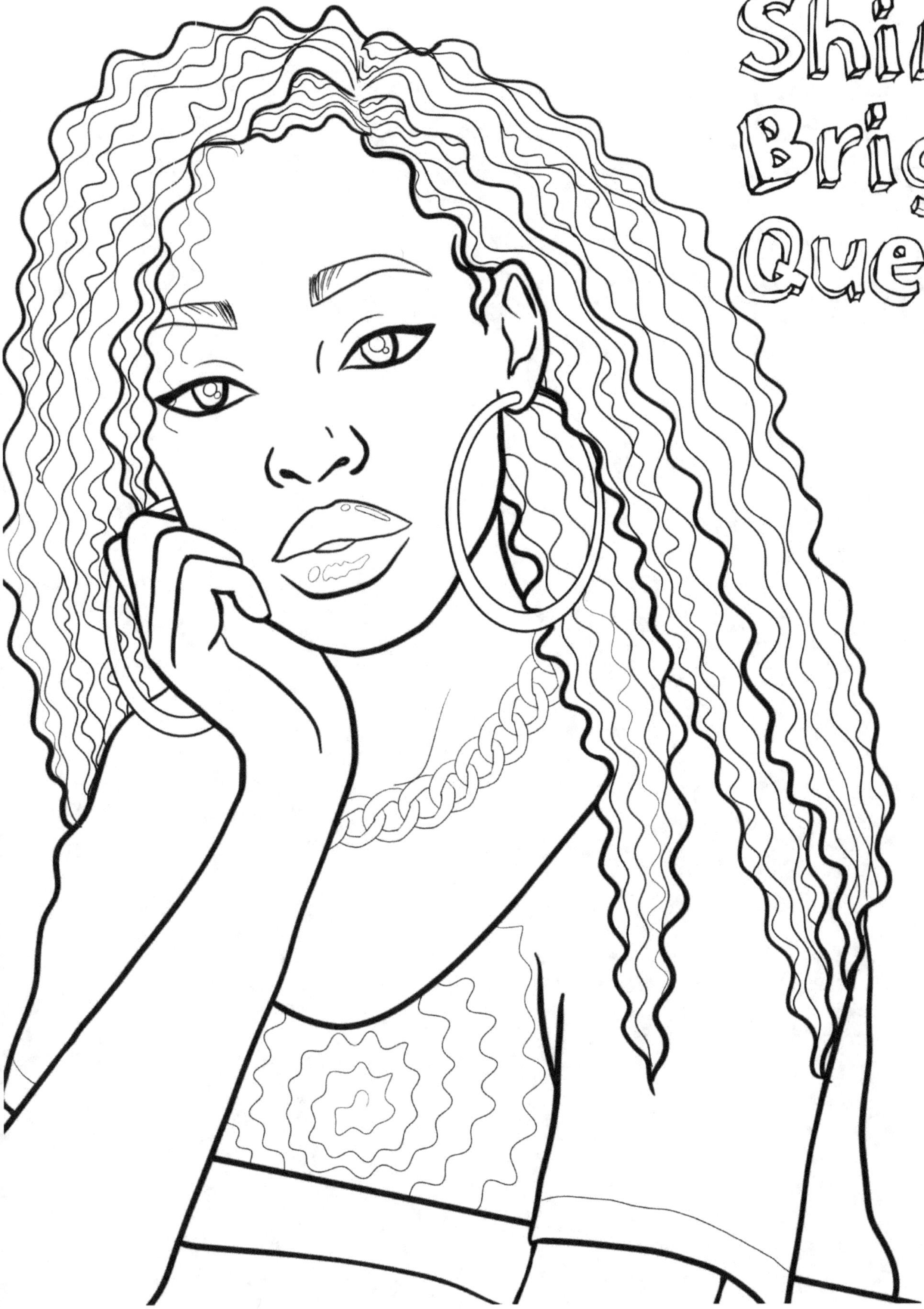

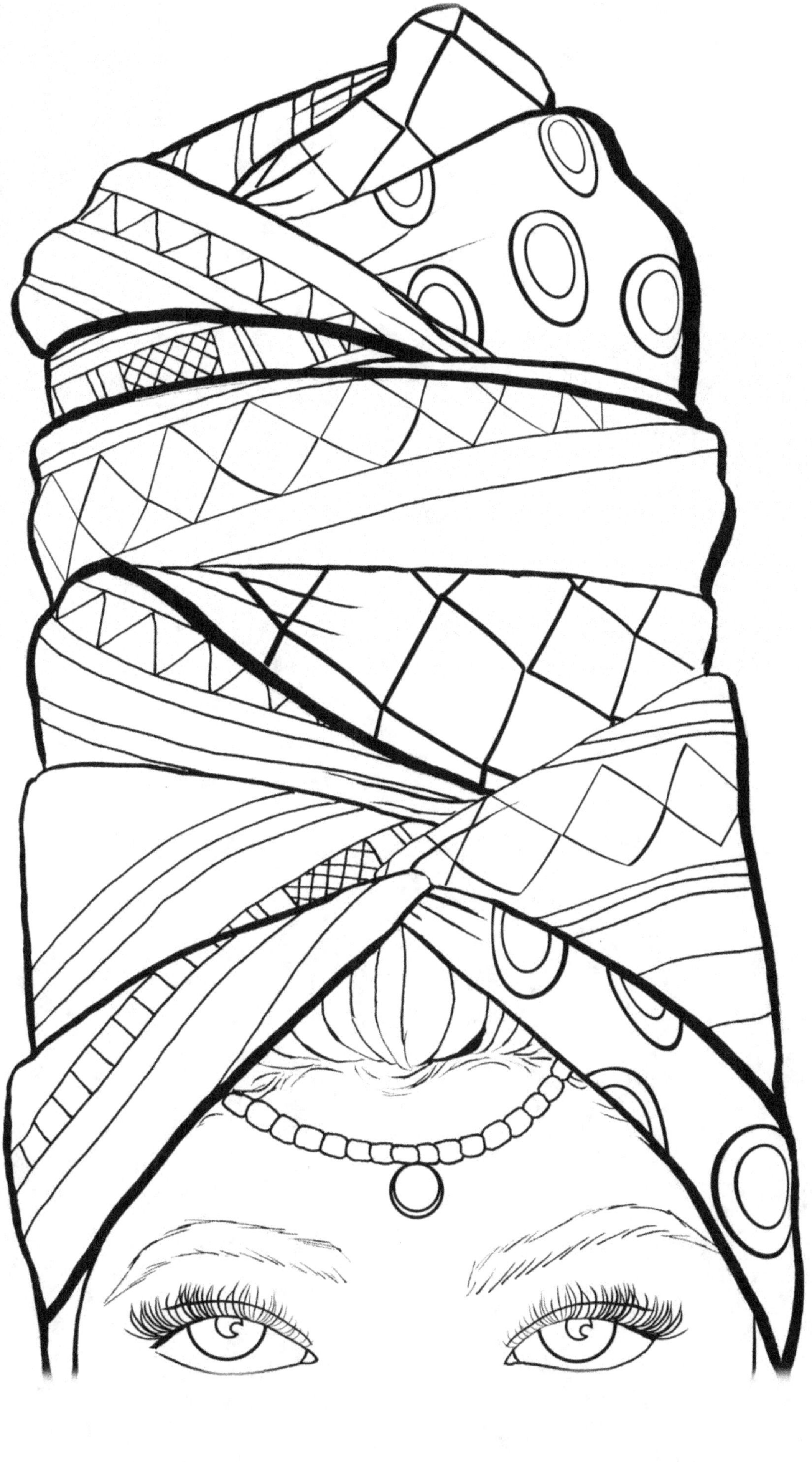

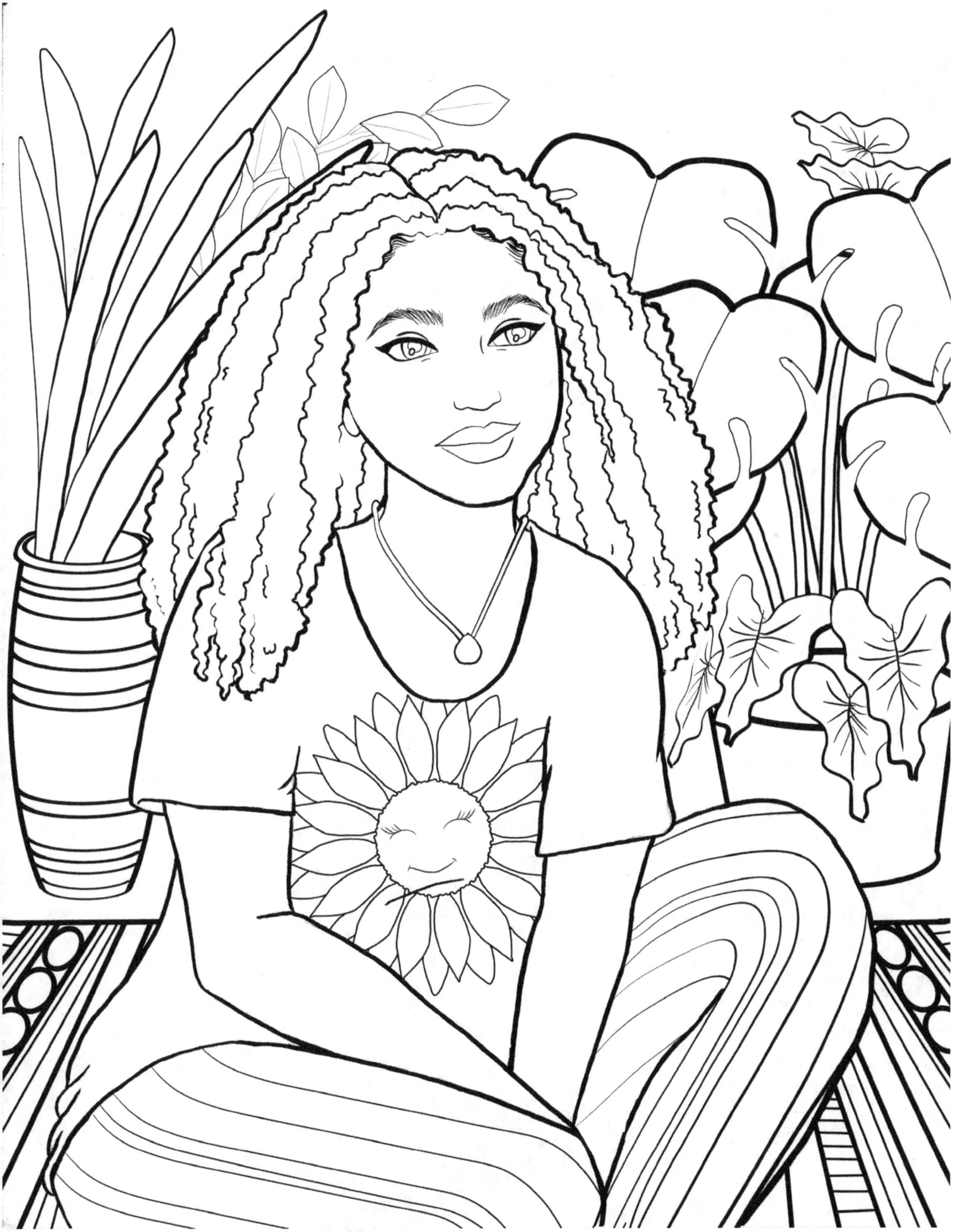

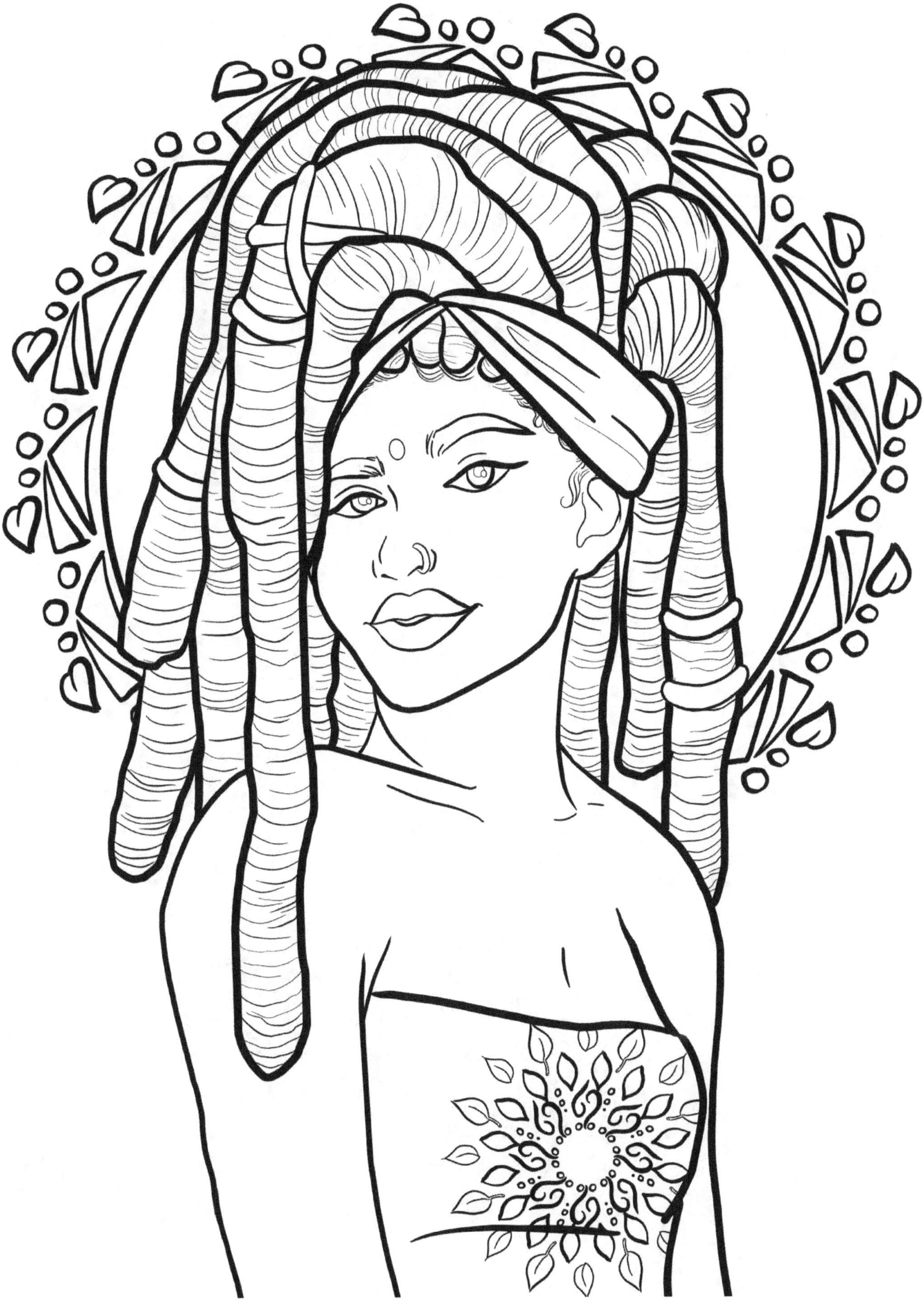

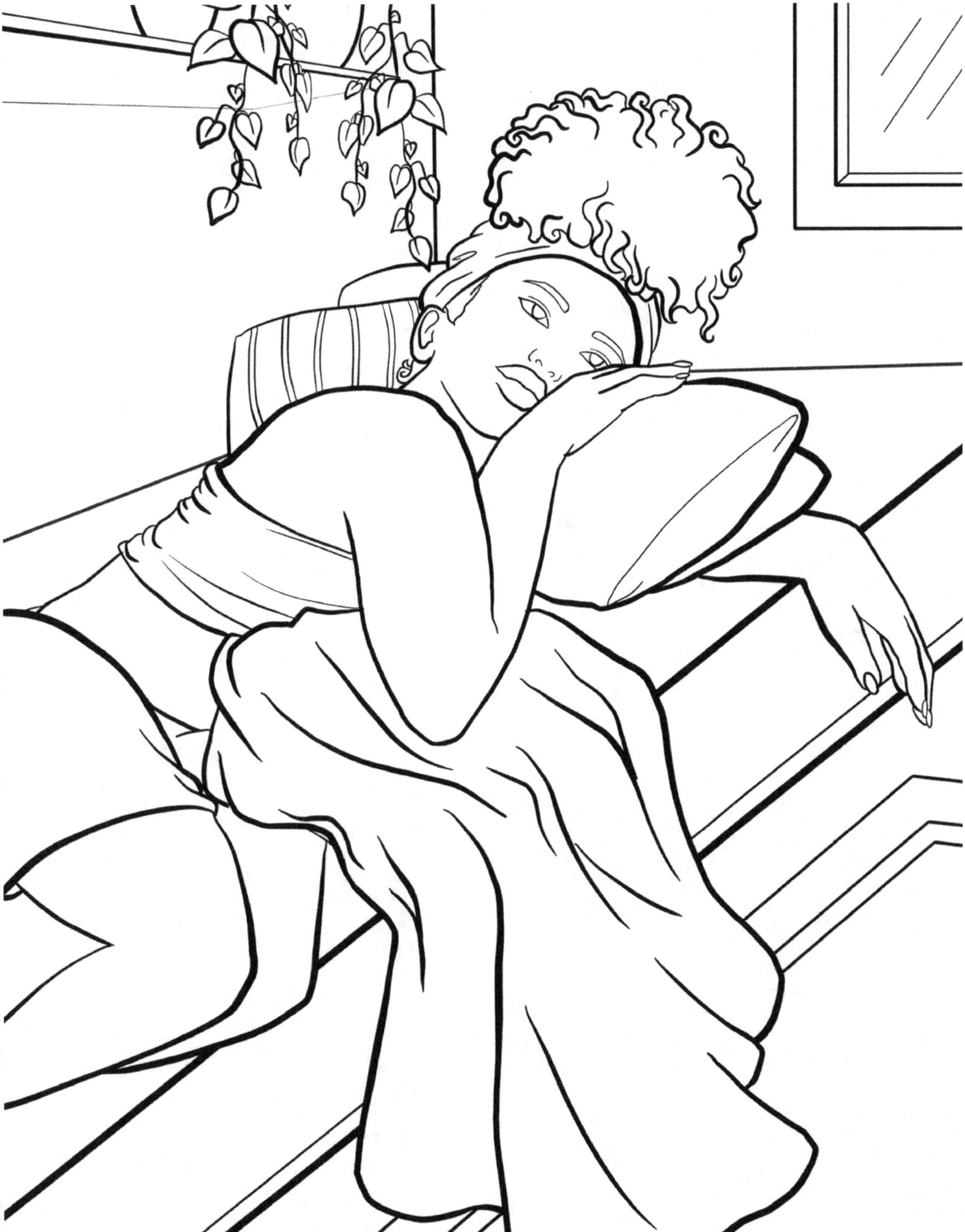

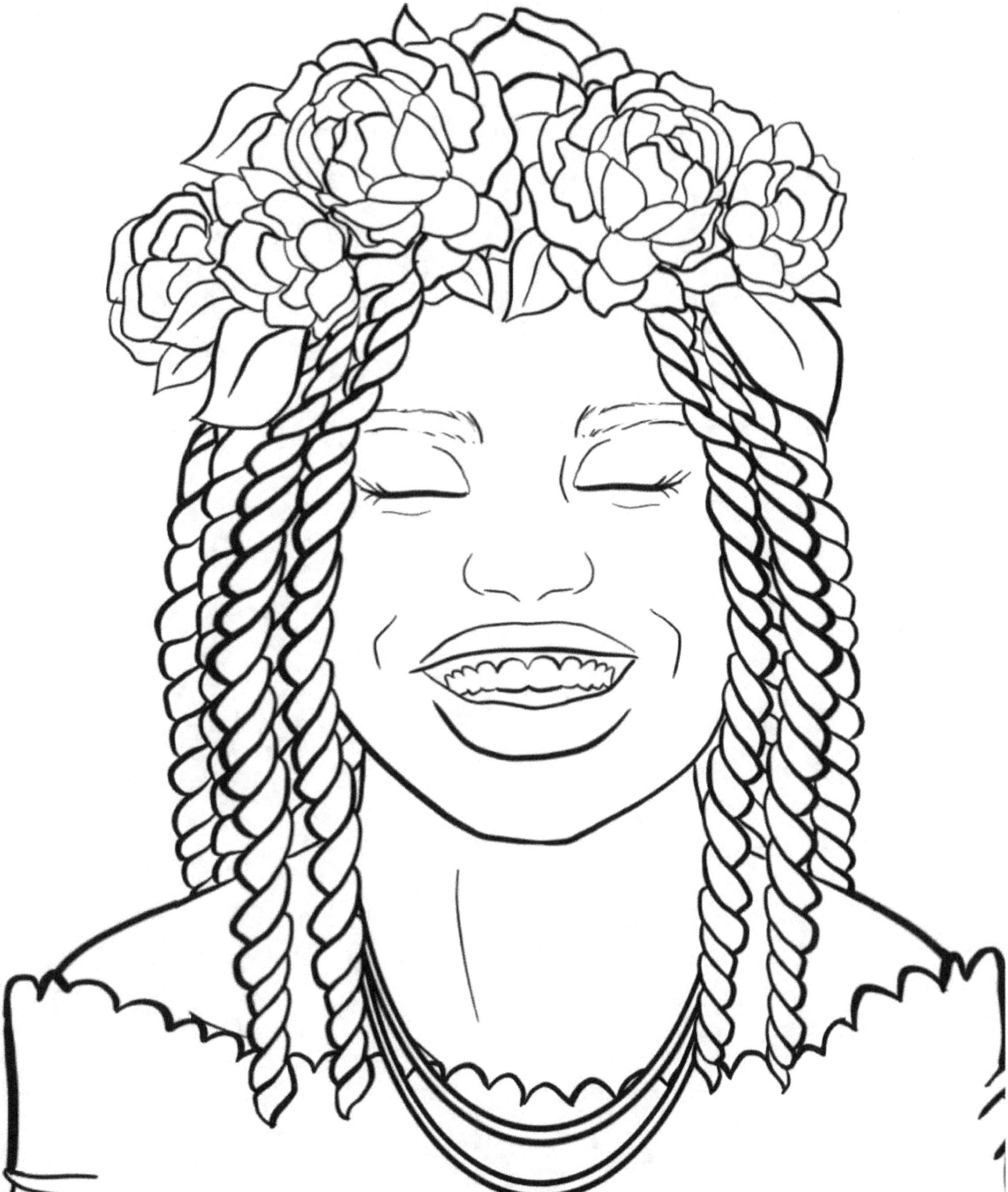

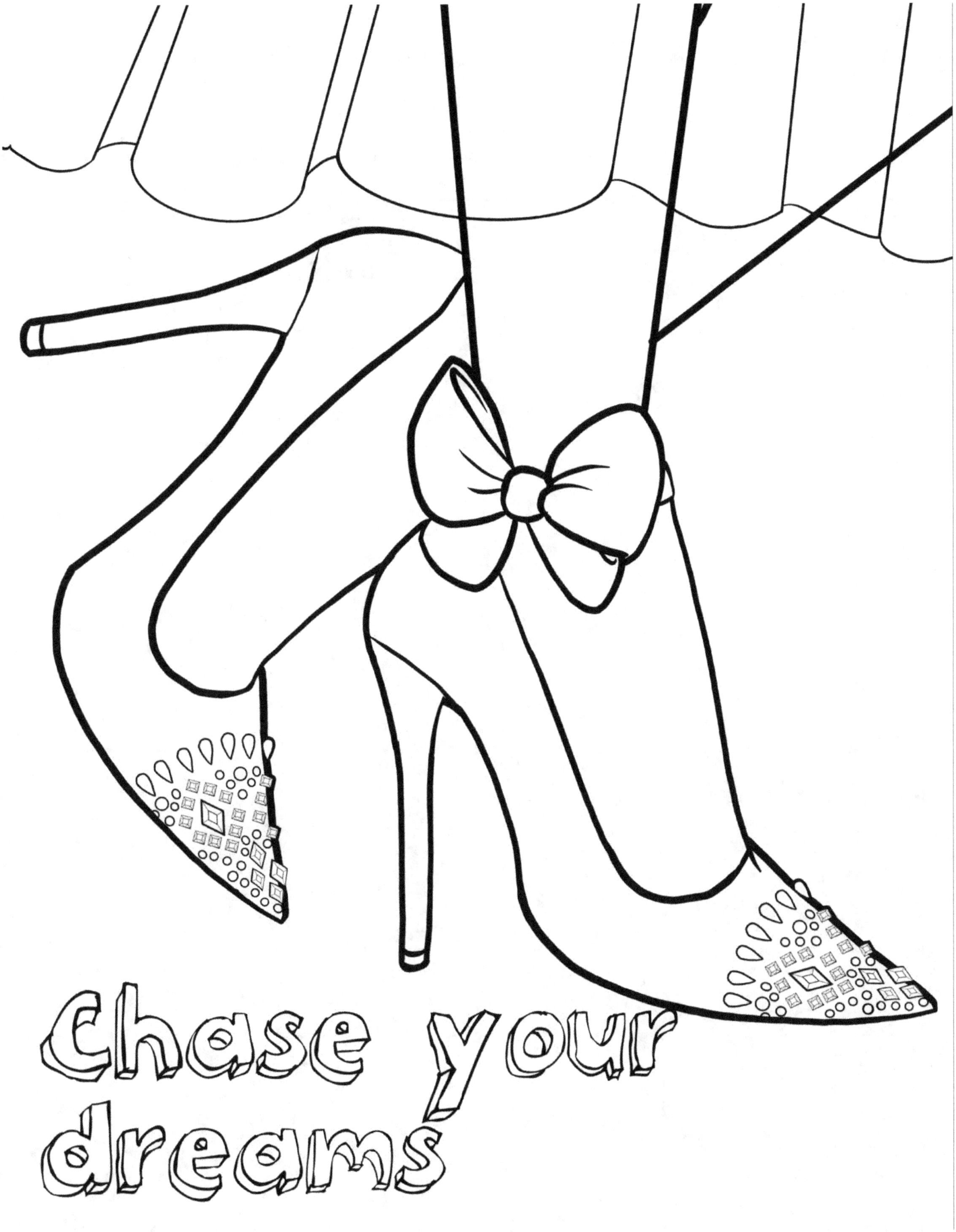

Chase your dreams

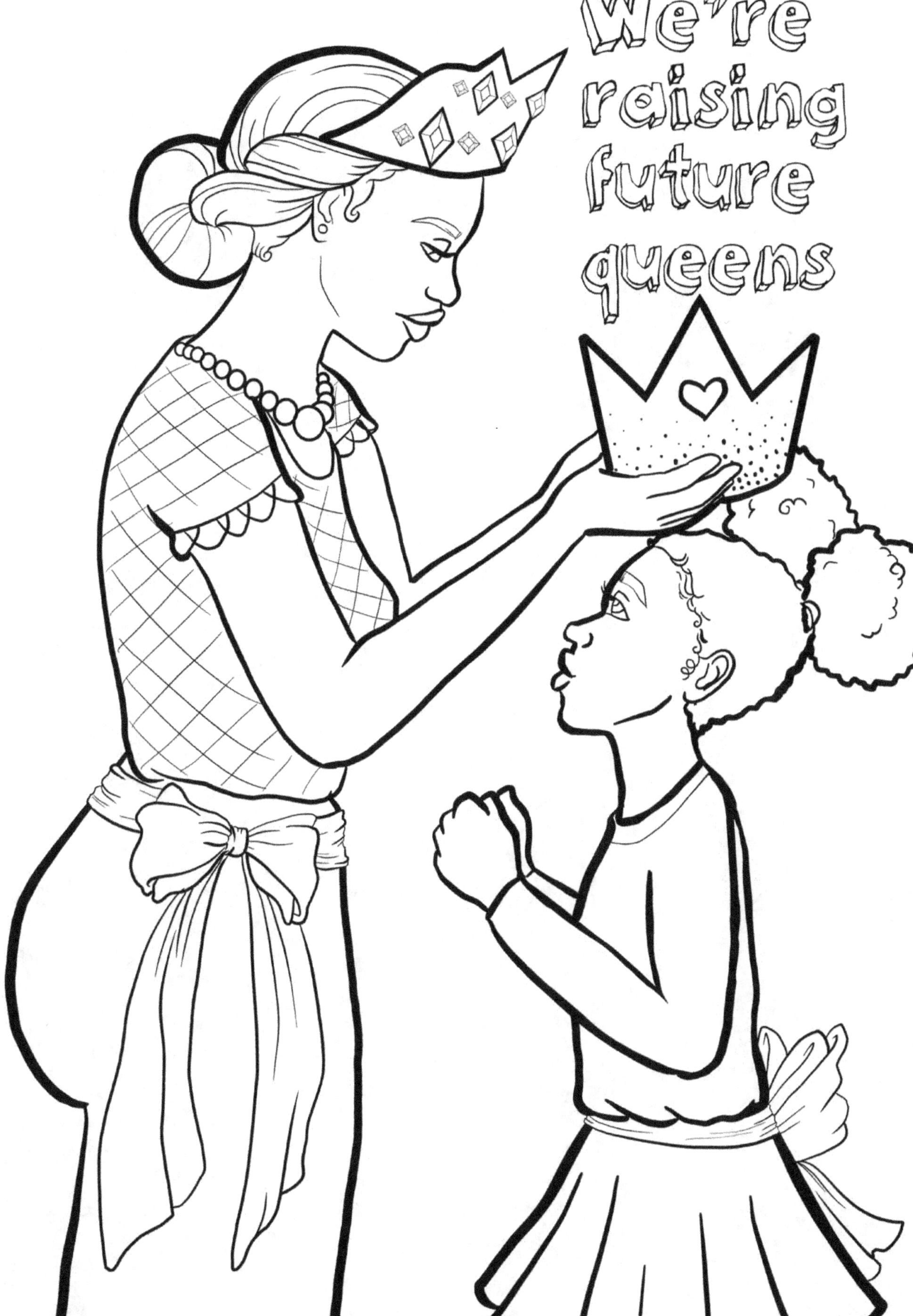
We're raising future queens

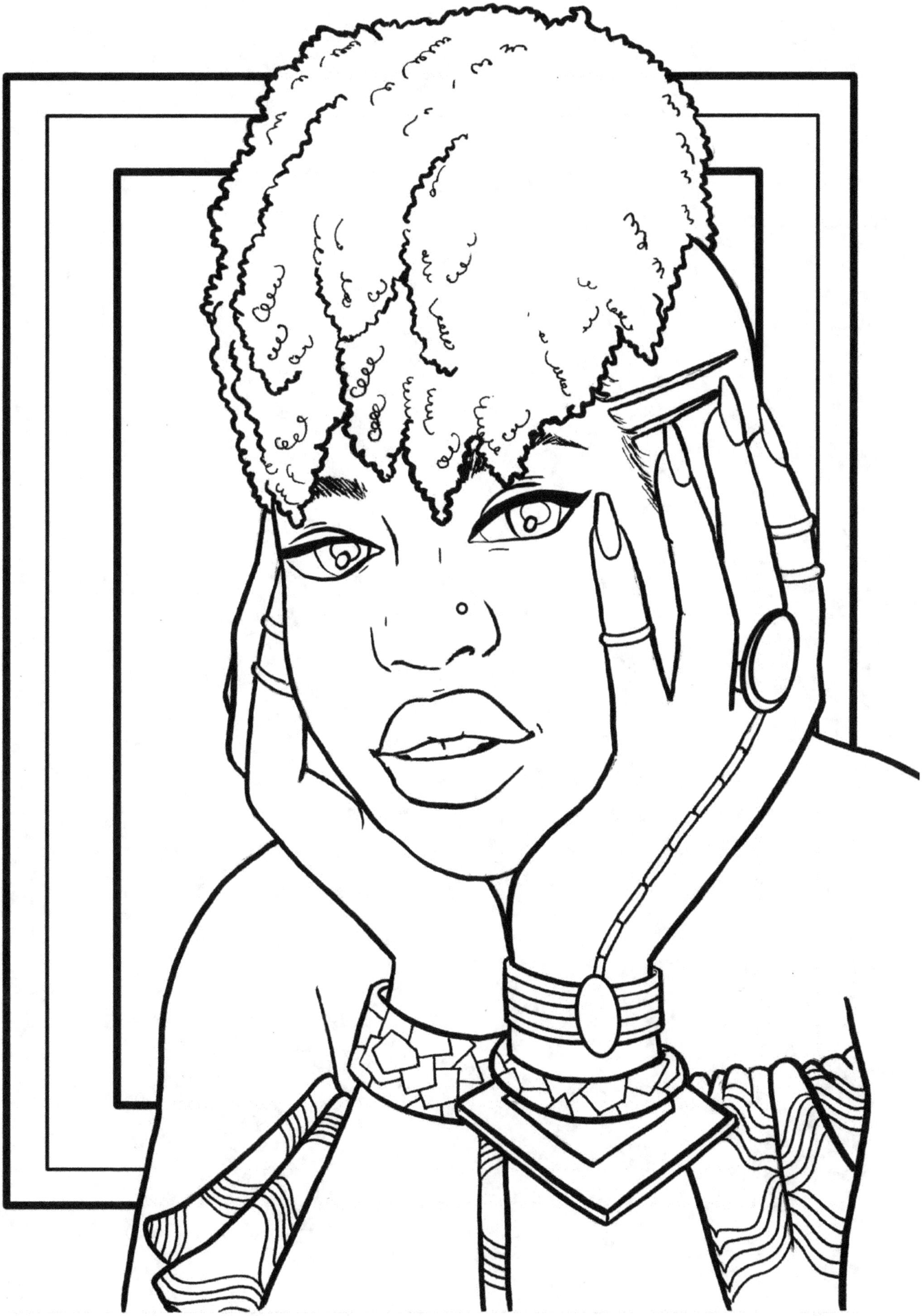

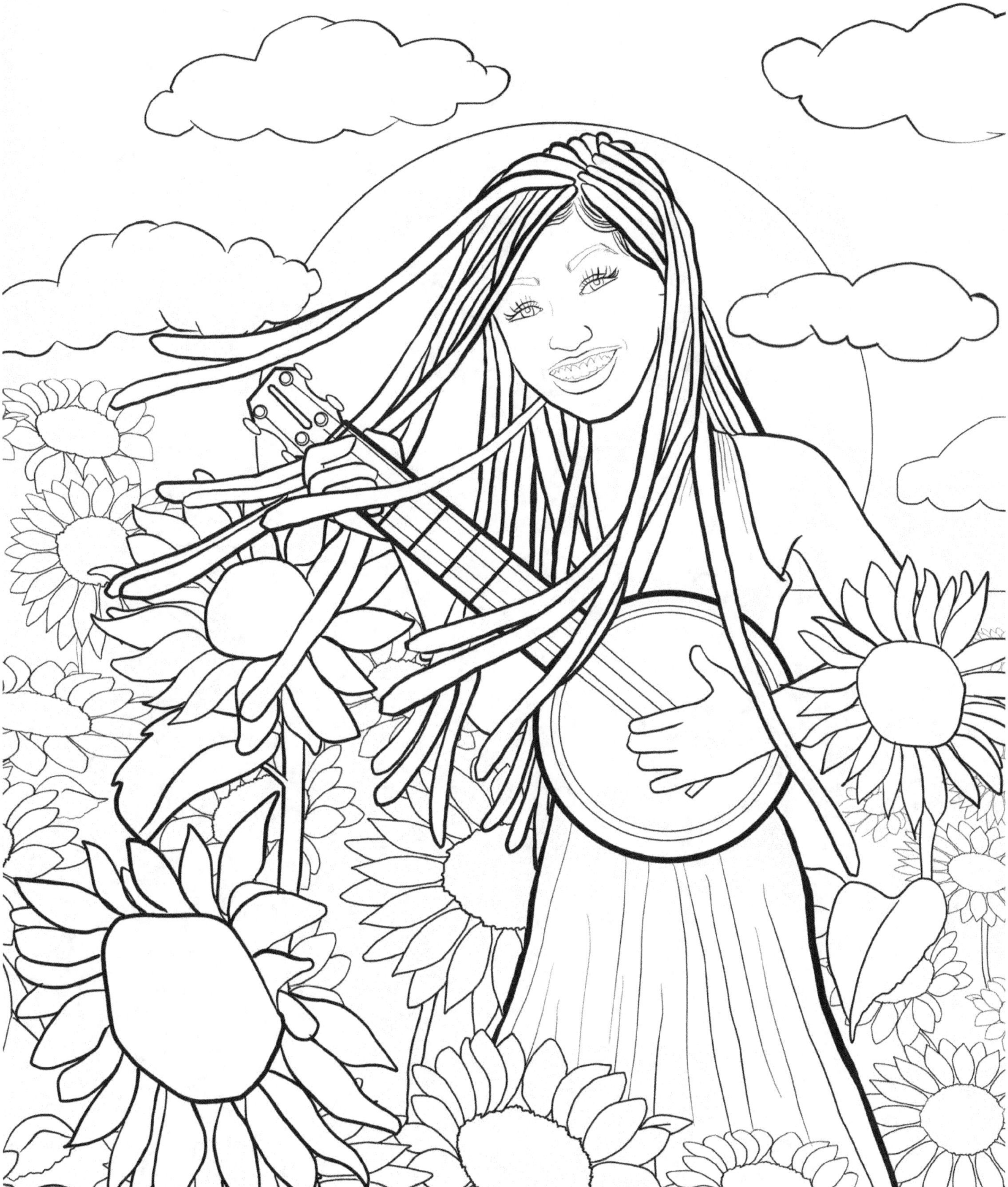

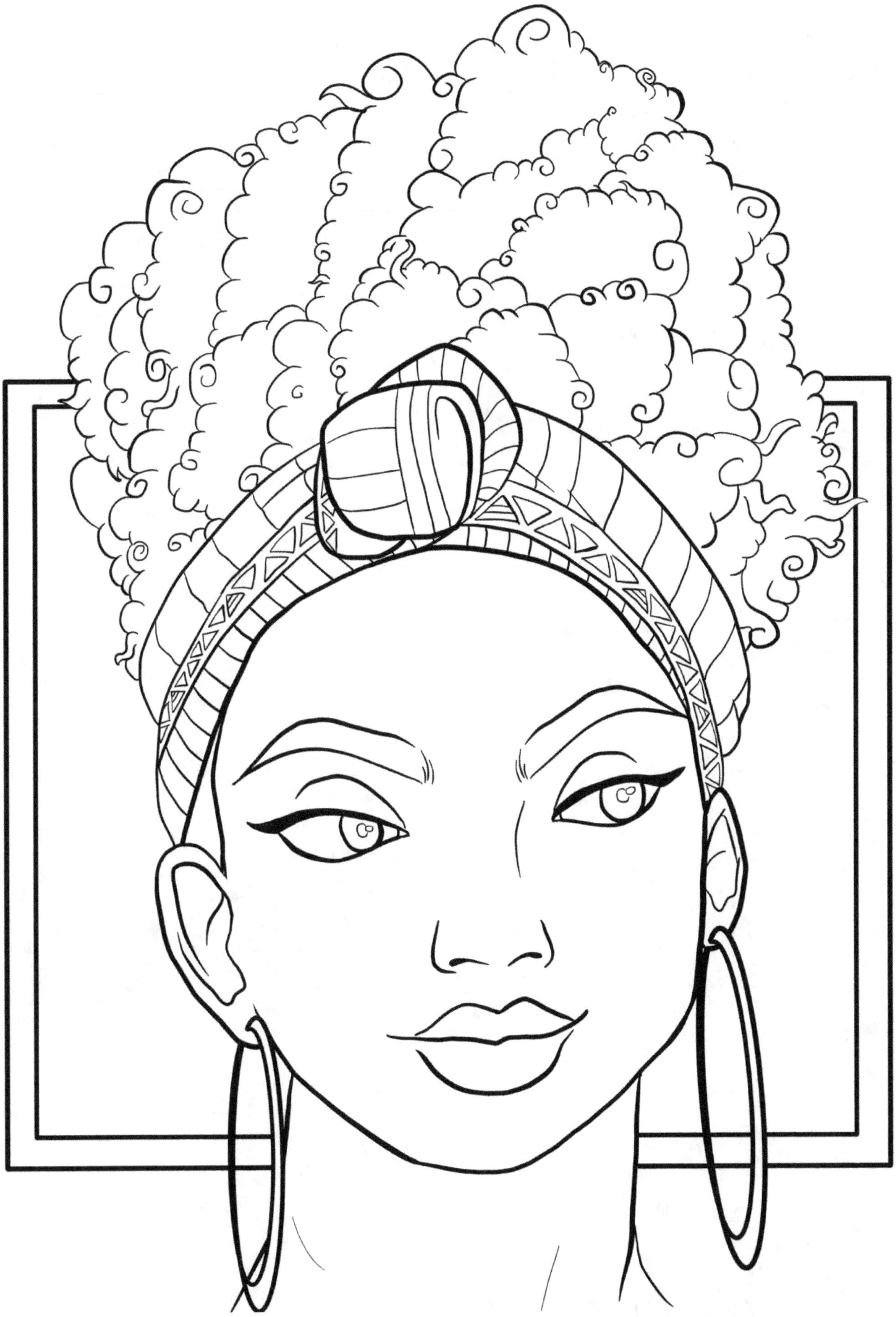

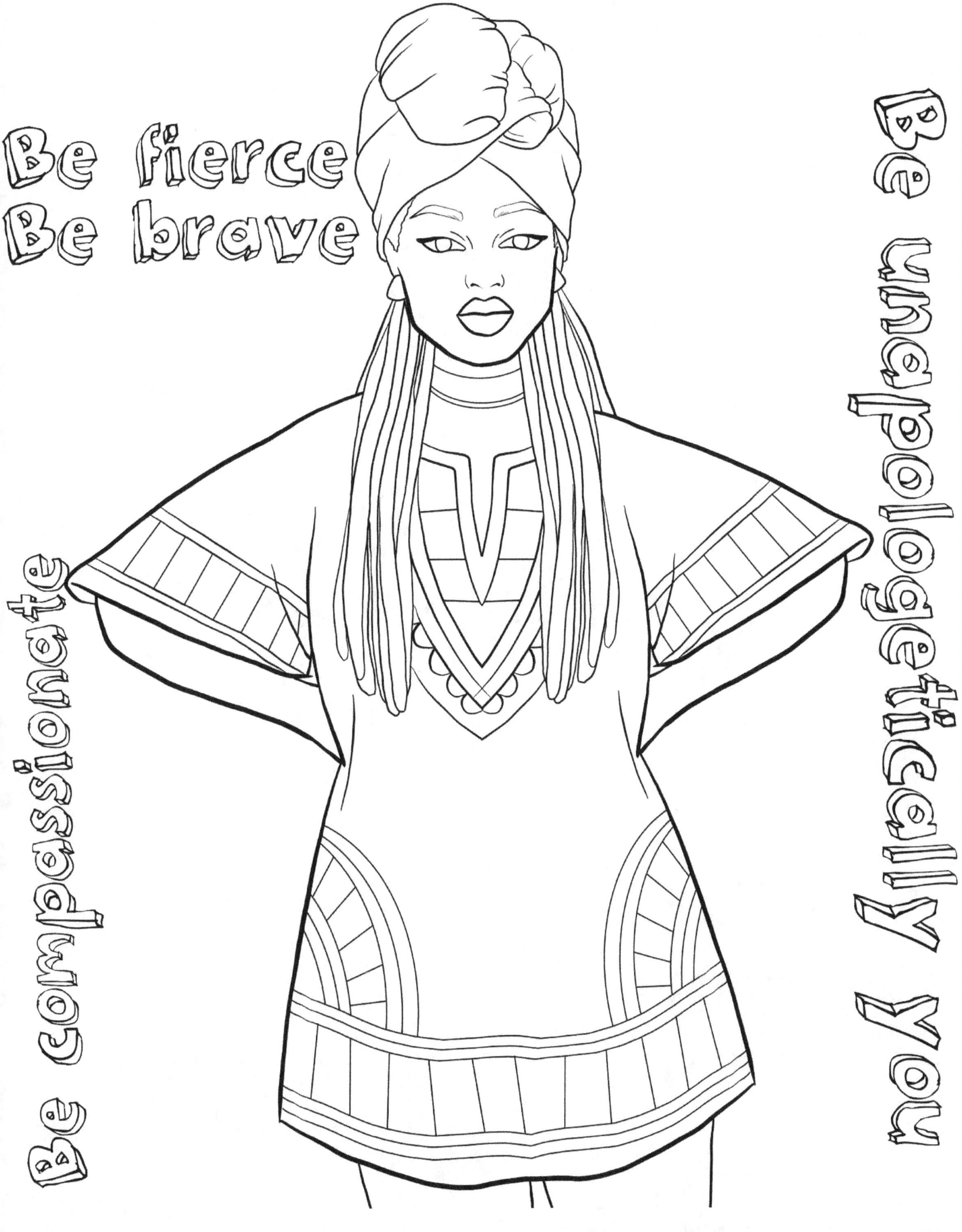
Be fierce
Be brave
Be compassionate
Be unapologetically you

Confidence
looks good
on you

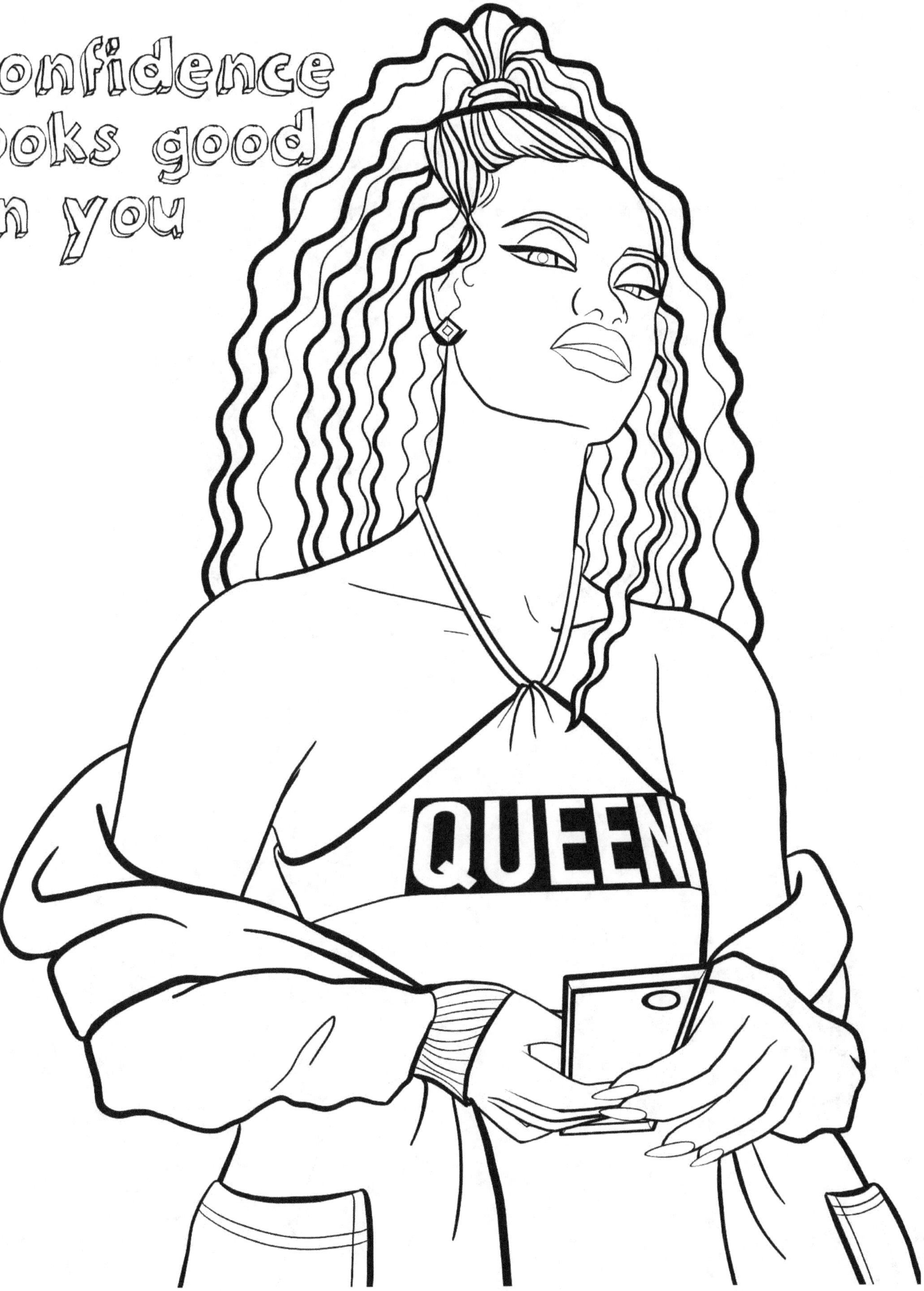

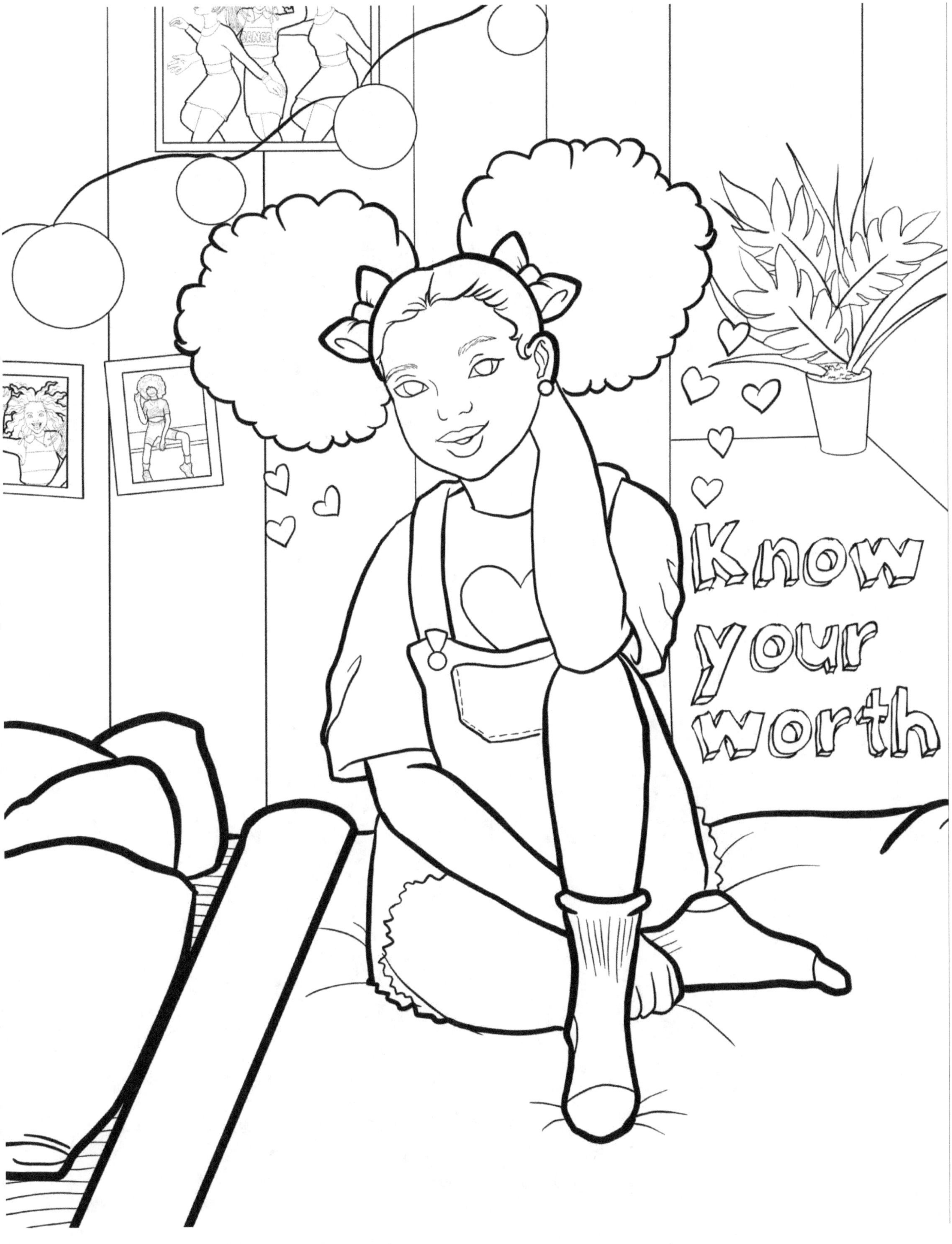
DANCE
Know your worth

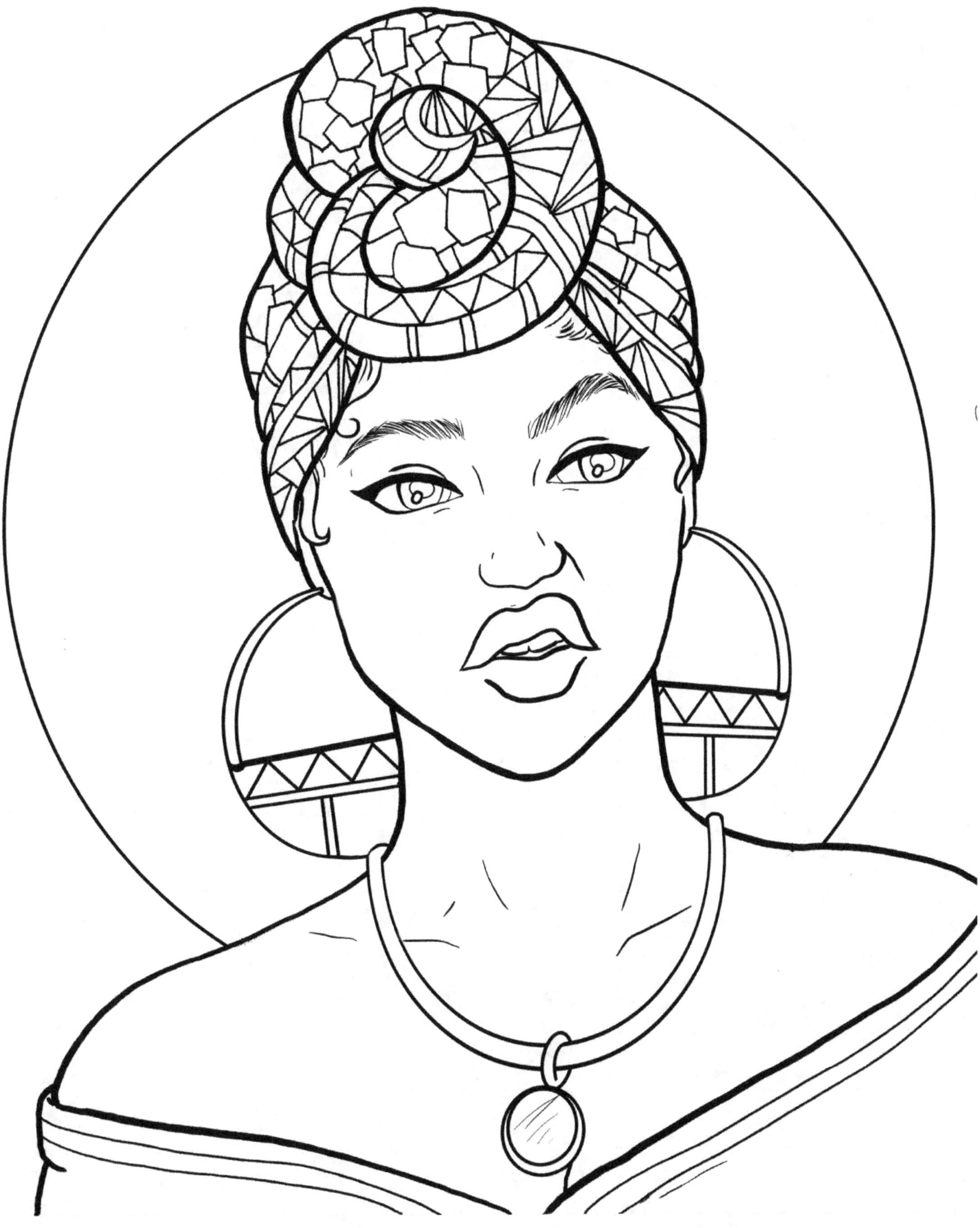

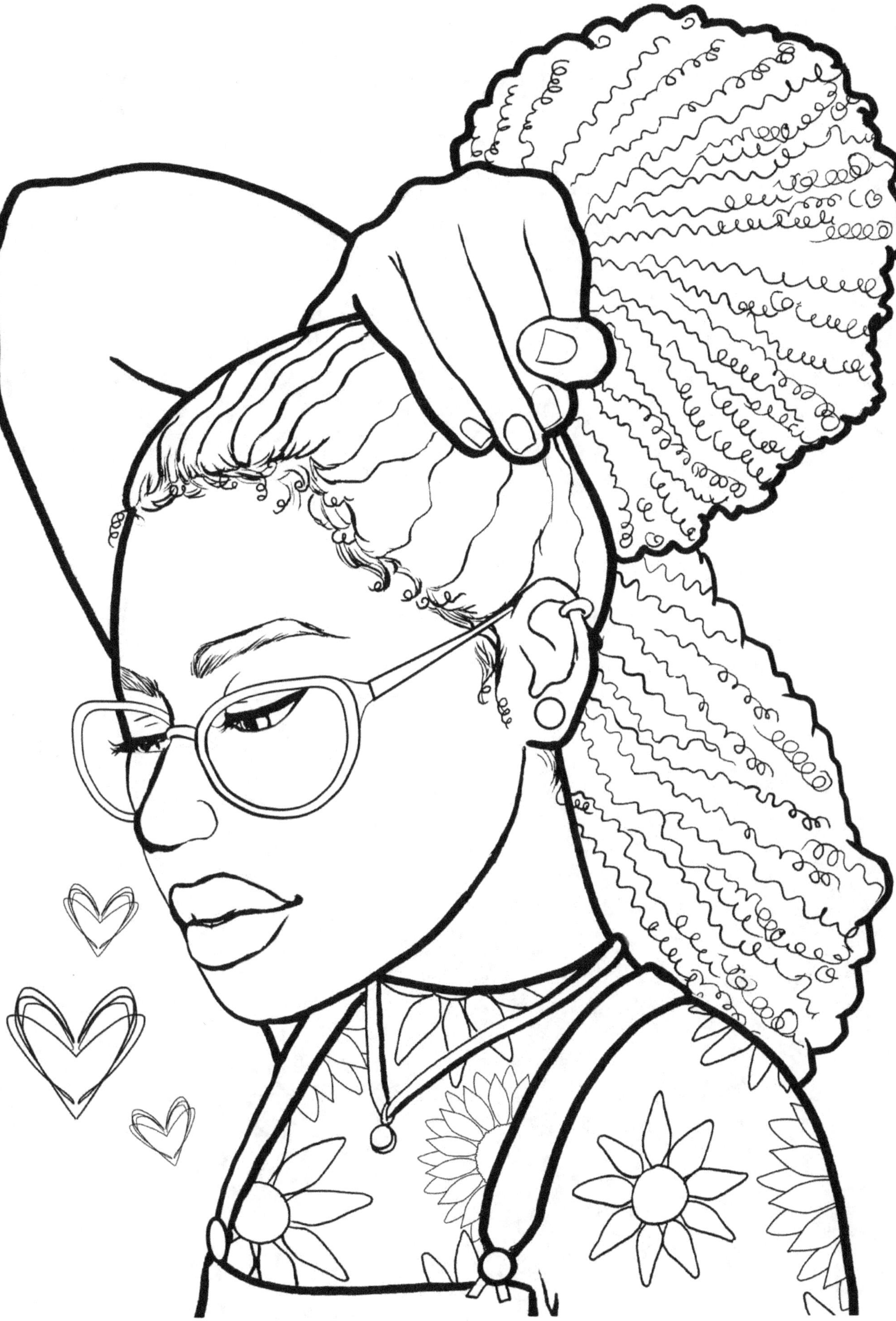

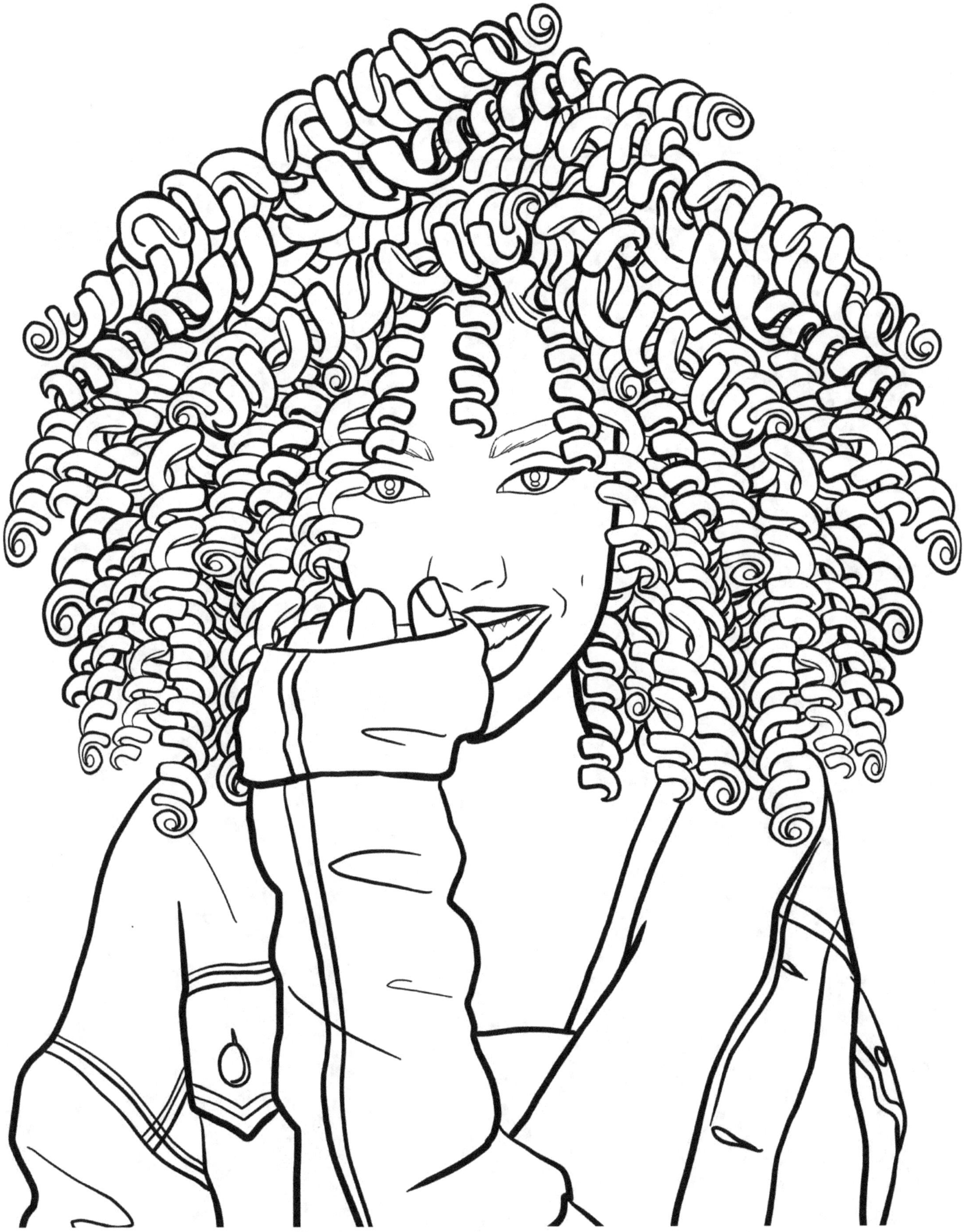

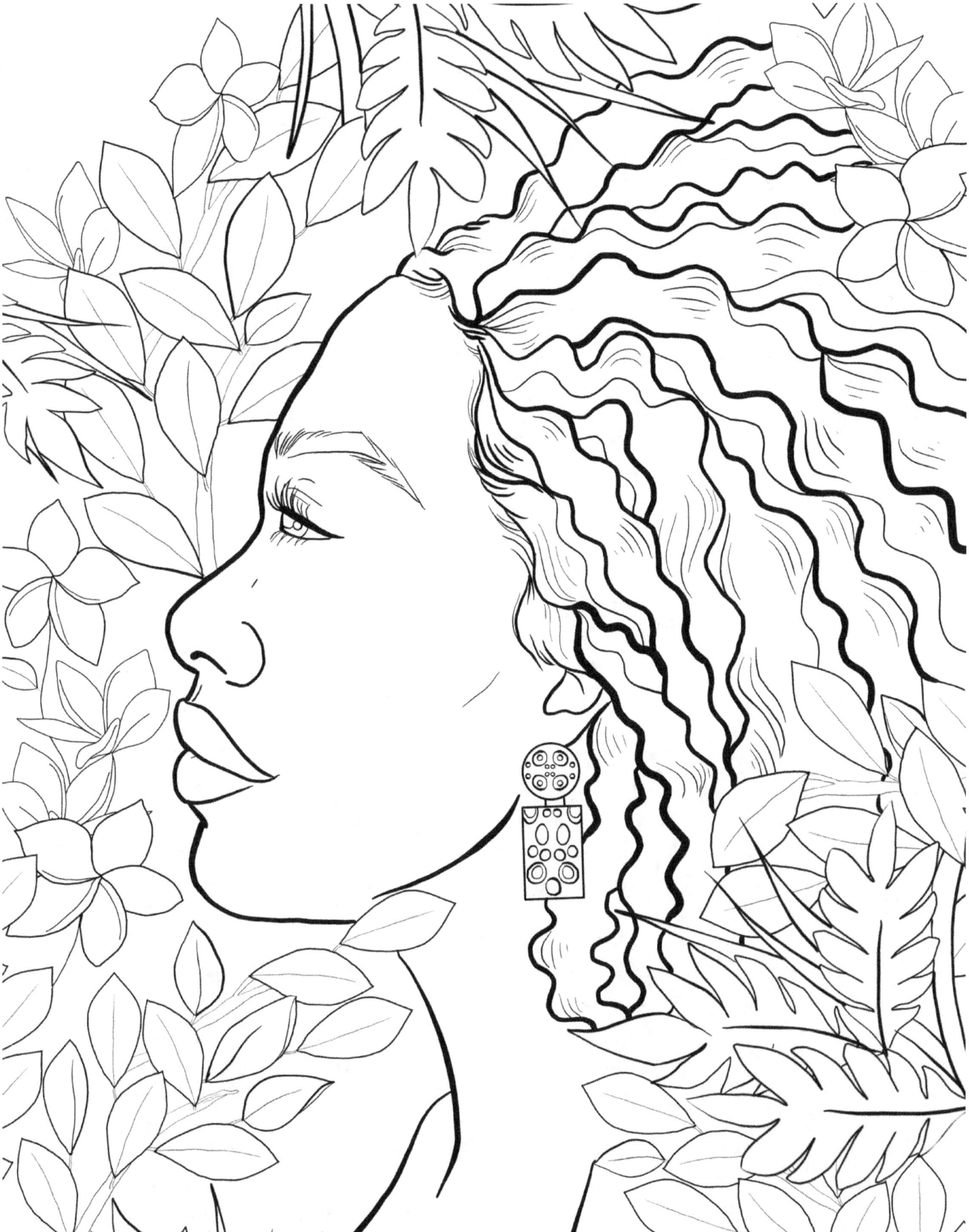

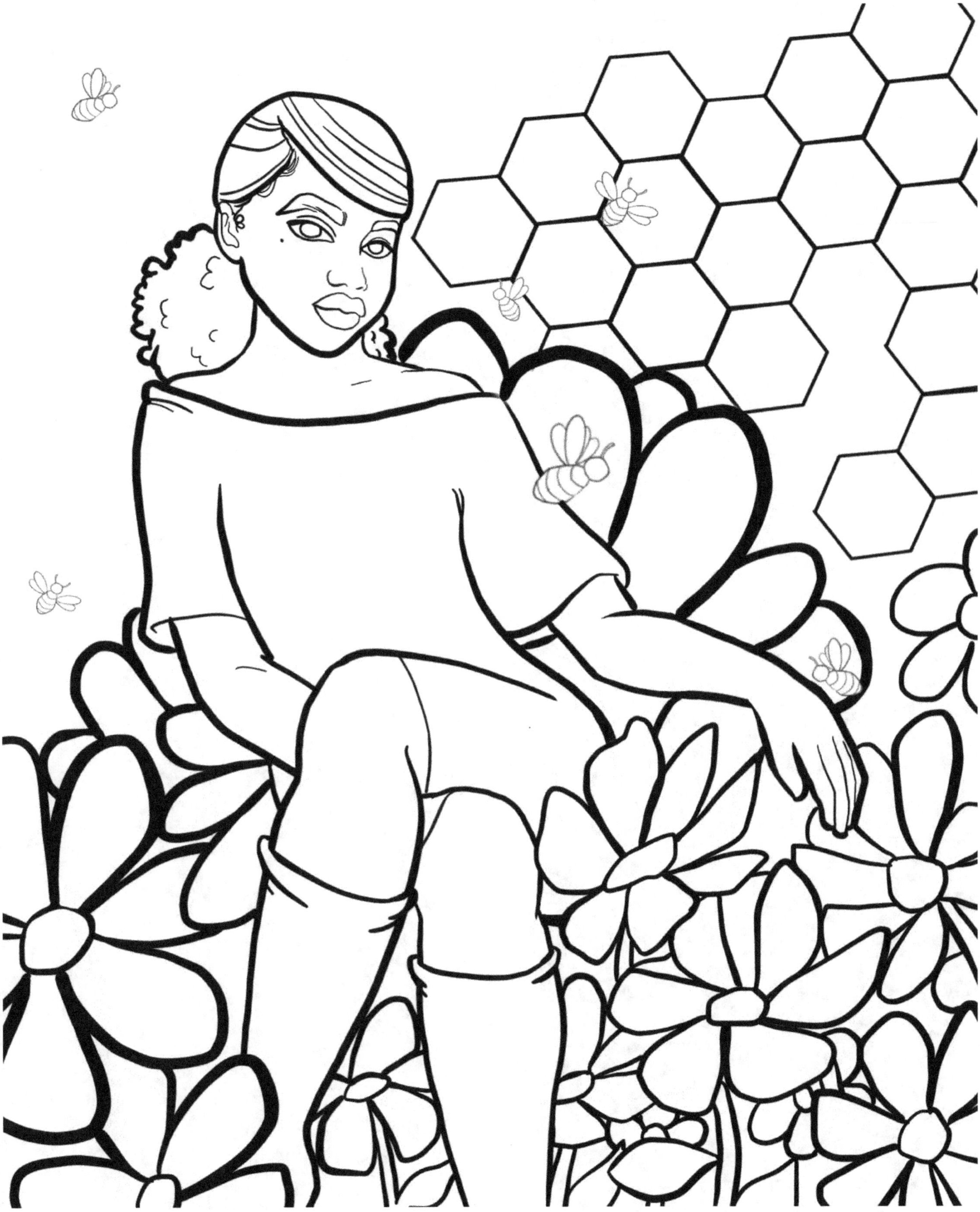

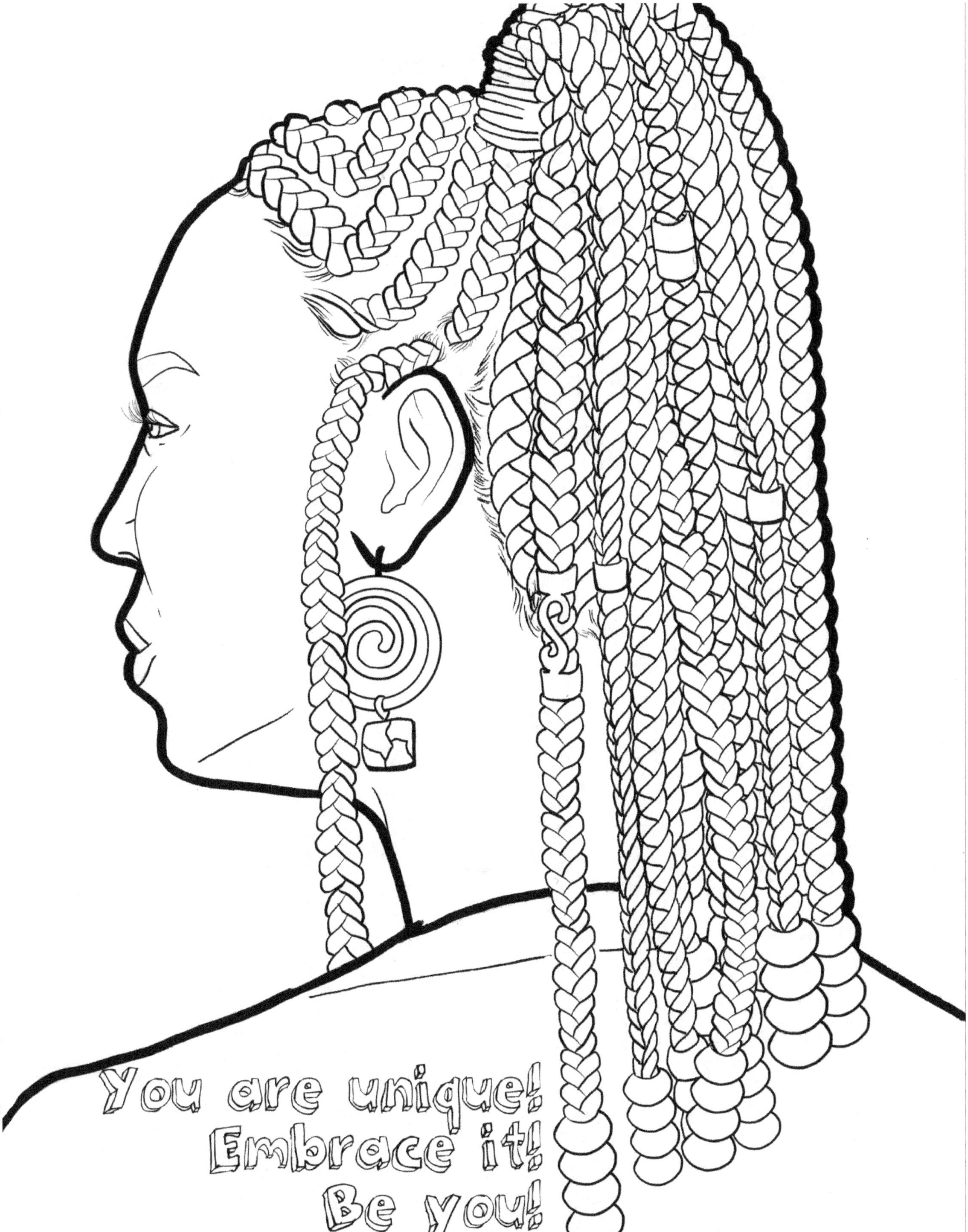
You are unique!
Embrace it!
Be you!

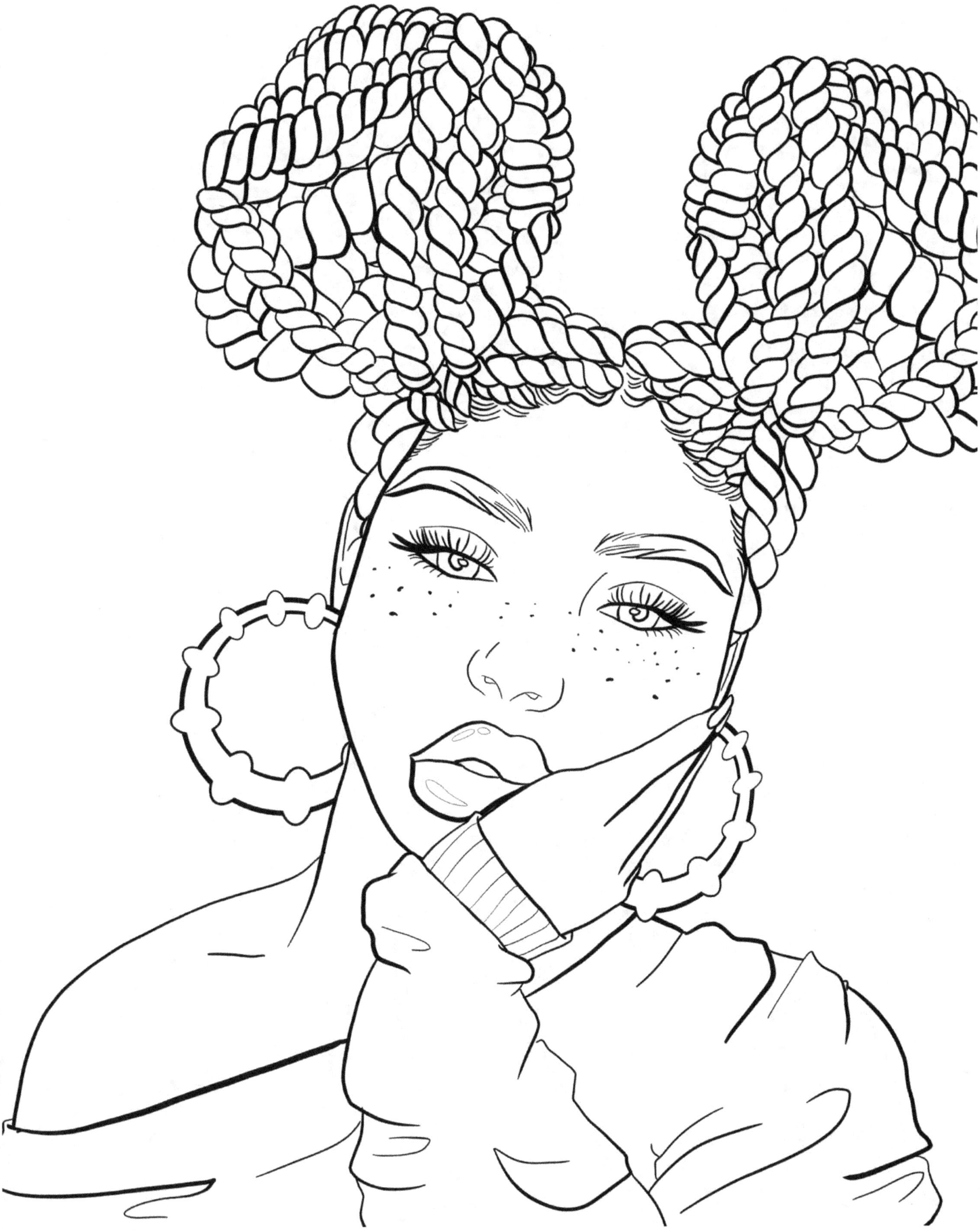

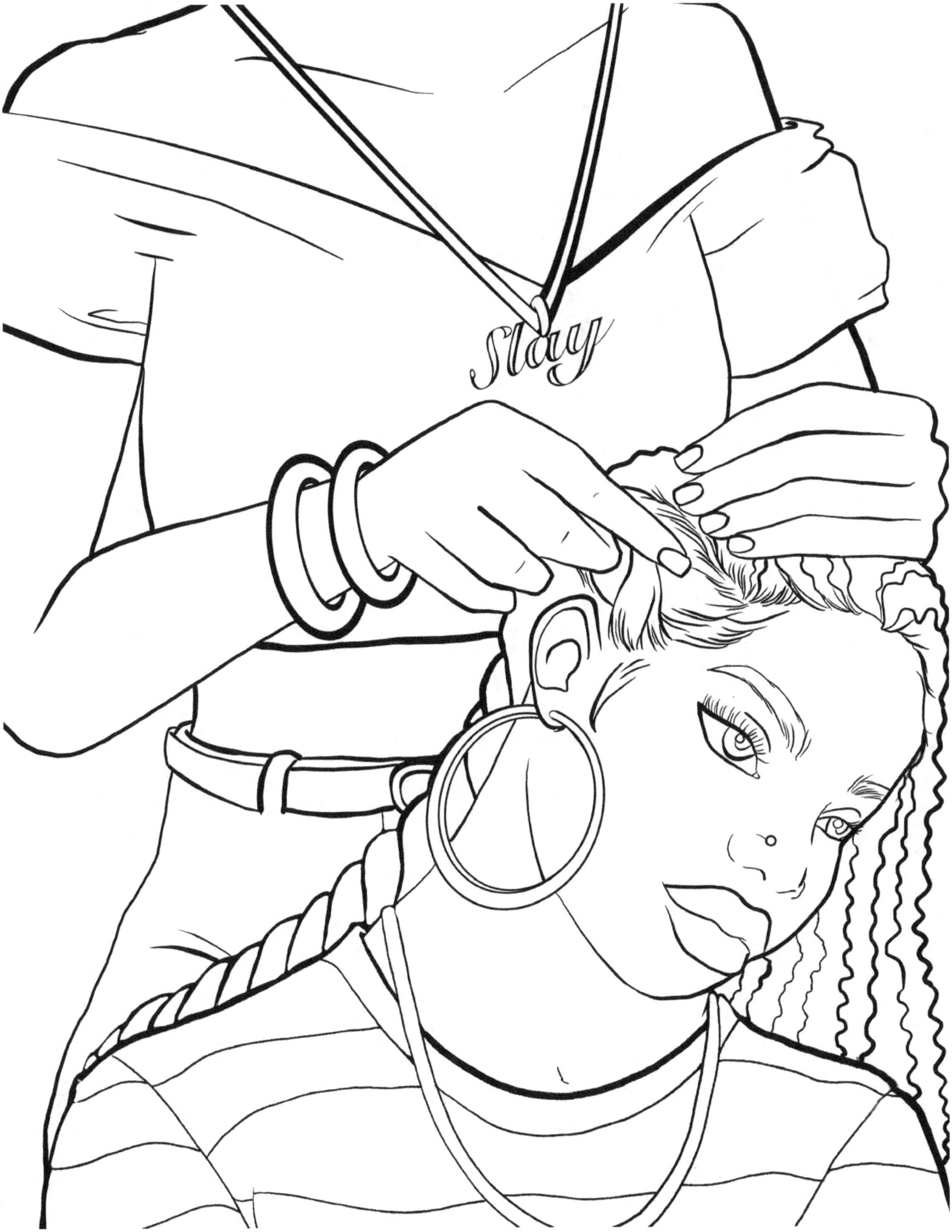
Slay

Cheers!

To you and all
of your
accomplishments,
I see you sis!
Keep going!

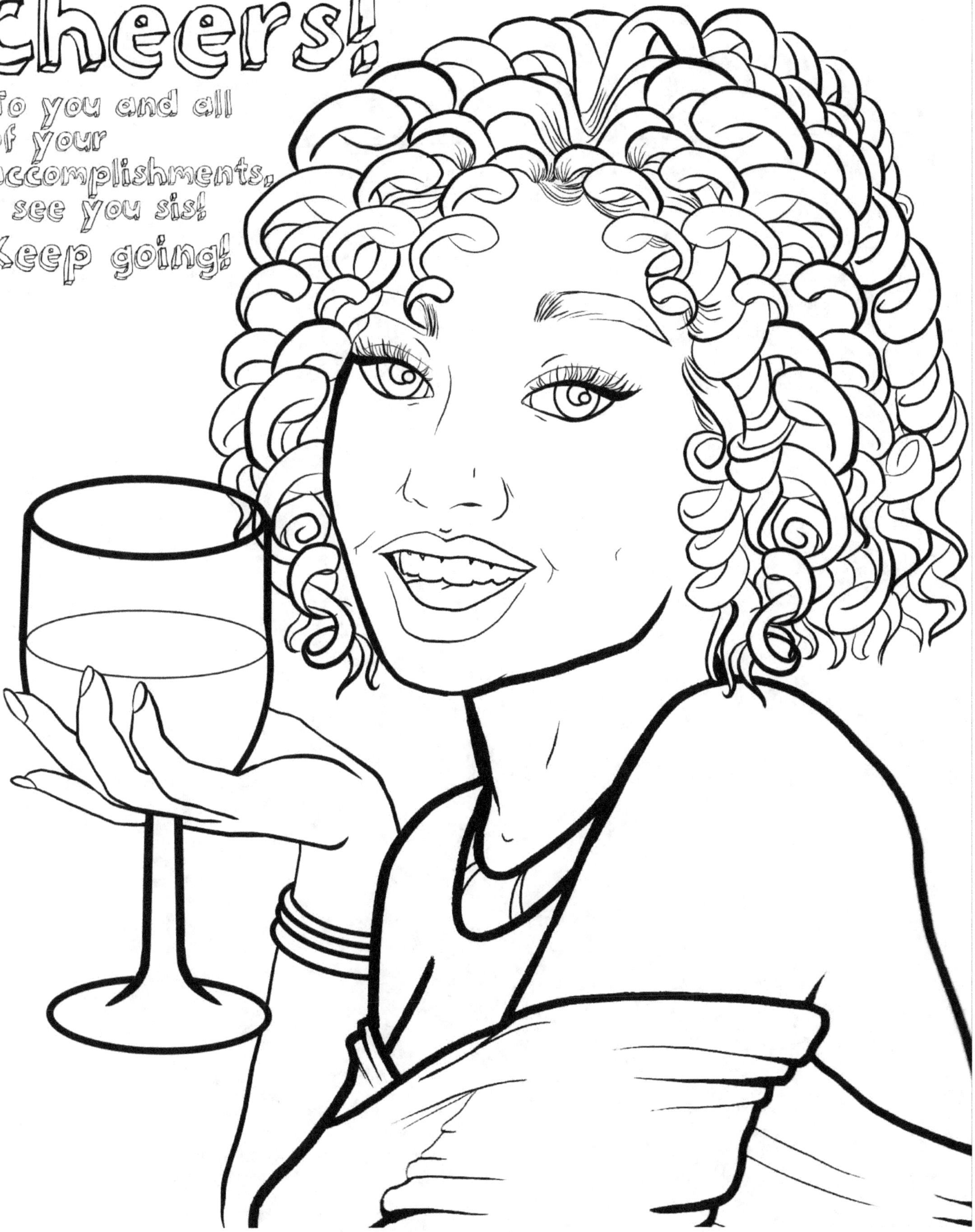

www.ingramcontent.com/pod-product-compliance
Lightning Source LLC
Chambersburg PA
CBHW080441220526
45465CB00007B/2729
* 9 7 9 8 6 5 0 9 6 9 7 1 6 *